OVEREATING: A DIALOGUE

OVEREATING: A DIALOGUE

An Application of the Principles of
A COURSE IN MIRACLES

KENNETH WAPNICK, Ph.D.

Foundation for A Course in Miracles®

Foundation for A COURSE IN MIRACLES®
41397 Buecking Drive
Temecula, CA 92590
www.facim.org

Copyright 1991, 1999 by the
Foundation for A COURSE IN MIRACLES®

Printed in the United States of America

Second printing 1993
Second edition 1999
Fourth printing 2001
Fifth printing 2004
Sixth printing 2008

Portions of *A Course in Miracles* copyright 1992,
Psychotherapy: Purpose, Process and Practice, copyright 1976, 1992
by the *Foundation for A COURSE IN MIRACLES*®

Library of Congress Cataloging in Publication Data

Wapnick, Kenneth
  Overeating : a dialogue : an application of the principles of A course in miracles / Kenneth Wapnick. -- 2nd ed.
    ISBN 0-933291-11-6
    1. Course in miracles. 2. Spiritual life. I. Title.
BP605.C68.W3596 1995
299'.93--dc20   95-51650

CONTENTS

Preface to Second Edition

We are presenting *Overeating* in book form, after its first nine years as a pamphlet. Aside from this new face and a few minor editorial revisions, the material remains unchanged.

Preface to First Edition

This book is a slightly edited transcript of a dialogue I had with three students of *A Course in Miracles* on April 28, 1990 at the Foundation's Academy and Retreat Center in Roscoe, New York. The students are Judith Beck, Betty Lipton, and Susan Peerless. The dialogue had its origin in the suggestion of Susan, a frequent participant in workshops at the Foundation. From time to time during these workshops, Susan would bring up the subject of her obsession with eating—hot fudge sundaes in particular—and in response I would relate her comments to various themes of the Course. Susan found these interactions helpful, and thought that a book on the subject of overeating and *A Course in Miracles* would be of great interest to Course students. I agreed, and suggested that we tape a discussion of the subject first, which could then become the basis for a pamphlet.

I believe that the taped discussion, and now this pamphlet, provide a good example of how the principles of *A Course in Miracles* may be applied to the understanding of specific symptomatology, in this case overeating. Such understanding, however, in and of itself does not heal, as the pamphlet *Psychotherapy: Purpose, Process and Practice** points out (P-2.VI.5 [see end of Preface for an explanation of this notation]). Nonetheless, dialogues such as this one can be helpful in the process of integrating the intellectual understanding of the Course with its personal application. The methodology reflected in this dialogue may therefore be generalized as well to other symptoms of guilt.

Except for minor and obvious stylistic corrections, the pamphlet is a faithful transcript of the original dialogue. Where comments have been added to clarify some of the statements made by the participants, it has been made clear to the reader through footnotes. The original ninety-minute audio tape of the dialogue is available from the Foundation for *A Course in Miracles*® for $6.00 (see Related Material at the end of the pamphlet for ordering information).†

---

* Foundation for Inner Peace (Mill Valley, CA 94942), 1976.

† Audio Tape discontinued. Available now in cd format. See Related Material at the end of the book for ordering information.

References to *A Course in Miracles* and the scribed pamphlet *Psychotherapy: Purpose, Process and Practice* correlate with the numbering system used in the recently published (1992-93) second editions. Examples follow:

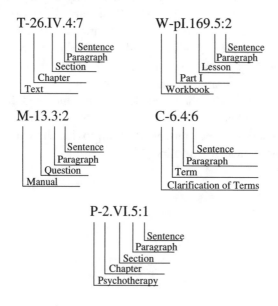

Acknowledgments

I am grateful to Susan for being the stimulus for this project (and actually transcribing the original audio tape), as well as to Judy and Betty for their willingness to be participants. Rosemarie LoSasso, the Foundation's Director of Publications, has done her usual conscientious and dedicated job in shepherding the project from start to finish for which, as always, I am very grateful. And to Gloria, my wife and the Foundation's Vice-President, I am indebted for—among her many helpful comments on the transcript—her wise recommendation to provide the explanatory notes which follow.

INTRODUCTION

The subtitle of the book is "An Application of the Principles of *A Course in Miracles*," and without some familiarity with the concepts of the Course—specifically its teachings on special relationships—the reader may find some of the statements made here to be irrelevant at best, and outrageous at worst. The format of the original dialogue did not include any in-depth theoretical explanation, as I presumed a basic understanding of the Course on the part of the participants, not to mention the expected audience. Therefore, some statements made were really the conclusions of a long sequence of ideas that were largely unverbalized. However, this book may end up reaching an audience, in part, that is relatively unfamiliar with *A Course in Miracles*. And so I shall preface the actual presentation with a brief summary of the Course's metaphysical teachings on specialness (the content) that are the foundation for the discussion on overeating (the form).[1]

In the dialogue, I refer to Helen Schucman and William Thetford, the two people responsible for the

---

1. For a more complete treatment of these ideas, the reader may consult *A Talk Given on A COURSE IN MIRACLES*, *Forgiveness and Jesus*, *Awaken from the Dream*, or *The Message of A COURSE IN MIRACLES* (see Related Material at the end of the book).

scribing of *A Course in Miracles*. Helen heard the voice of Jesus dictating the Course to her, and was assisted in the seven-year process of scribing by Bill, her colleague and close friend.[2]

Separation, Specialness, and Overeating: Content and Form

A Course in Miracles teaches that the basis of the entire physical universe, not to mention our experience as physical and psychological beings, is the belief that we have actually separated from God, our Creator and Source. This thought, which the Course stresses is illusory, consists of the dynamics of *sin* (the belief that the separation truly occurred), *guilt* or self-hatred (being the psychological experience of sin), and *fear* (of our expected punishment by God that is the inevitable consequence of sin and guilt). This unholy trinity of sin, guilt, and fear is the foundation of the ego's thought system that we fabricated as the content of our nightmare dream. Through the dynamic of projection, this dream evolved into the making of the world of form as a defense against the

---

2. The full story of the Course's dictation can be found in *Absence from Felicity: The Story of Helen Schucman and Her Scribing of A Course in Miracles* (see Related Material at the end of the book).

imagined wrath of God. Thus we held the magical hope that this defense would be a fortress to keep God's vengeful love, an already mistaken concept, away from us. The Course states:

> The world was made as an attack on God. It symbolizes fear. And what is fear except love's absence? Thus the world was meant to be a place where God could enter not, and where His Son could be apart from Him (W-pII.3.2:1-3).

The world and body, therefore, come to embody this thought of separation, since, as the Course emphasizes, what is perceived to be outside our minds is merely the reflection or projection of what is within: the inner and outer being the same. We may think of ourselves sitting in a movie theater, where what is perceived as real (psychologically at least) on the movie screen is simply the projection of a film that is running through the film projector. Moreover, it is impossible that there be anything on the screen that has not been projected from the film in the projector (or that is on the lens of the projector), nor anything on the film (or lens) that will not be projected onto the screen. This is analogous to the situation regarding the thoughts (the film) that are in our minds (the film projector), which are directly responsible for our experiences in the physical world (what is perceived on the movie screen).

Therefore, to summarize it very simply: what we perceive, do, feel, and think with our bodies is nothing more than the reflection of our minds' underlying thoughts. Observing what we do can therefore help us to understand the contents of our separated minds, which, incidentally, should not be confused with our brains, which are simply part of the body. Similarly, understanding the basic dynamics of the ego thought system will help us to understand better the meaning of our bodily activities.

From the perspective of the ego, the thought of separation is a horrifying idea. To make the point again, the ego's dream, as the Course characterizes the illusory ego world, upholds the belief that we have usurped the place of God, in effect killing Him, having stolen His Love, Power, and Life. Upon this murdered Self of God we believe we have erected our own triumphant self, now become all-powerful because of what it has cannibalized from its Creator. This separated self, called "the ego" by the Course, exists only because of what it stole, without which it would simply cease to be.

From its inception, therefore, the ego's existence is dependent on the God it has perceived to be outside it, from Whom it has stolen its very "life." This experience of lack threatens the ego's existence, and it must therefore continually attempt to "feed off" this source of "life" by re-enacting the original rape of Heaven, another way of conceiving the thought of separation. This ongoing ego need to steal from the outside to sustain its own existence is what the Course refers to as "specialness": the need to meet one's *special* needs by cannibalizing *special* people who are perceived as possessing the *specialness* we require to live our lives.

Returning now to the principle that what is within our minds is projected out, we can better understand the nature of the body, which again is simply the out-picturing of the mind's thought. A body—the expression in form of the ego's thought of separation and specialness—cannot exist without cannibalizing an external energy source. Thus, without taking in food from the outside—through killing what seemed to be alive and then eating it—the body will starve to death; also, without breathing in oxygen, the body would die as well. We therefore can understand that buried in the unconscious minds of everyone is the symbolic connection that with every morsel we ingest, with every breath we take, we are re-enacting the original separation thought. As the Course teaches more abstractly:

> Each day, and every minute in each day, and every instant that each minute holds, you but relive the single instant when the time of terror took the place of love (T-26.V.13:1).

Believing ourselves to be physical beings, we thus relive this terrible instant every second of our lives.

This metaphysical background also helps to explain why almost all people walking this earth experience some conflict, anxiety, or problem surrounding food, not to mention having the varied associations of specialness that inevitably arise around eating. This clearly does not mean that we should feel guilty each time we eat or breathe. But an understanding of how and why the ego made the world in general, and the body specifically, is helpful in understanding exactly what the ego thought system is. Until we develop the film in our cameras, we do not really know what is on the film. Without knowing what we have to change in our minds, it is impossible to do so.

A Course in Miracles teaches that our minds have a choice between the ego's thought system of specialness and the Holy Spirit's thought system of forgiveness. The former is based on the belief that the separation from God actually occurred, as we have already seen, while the latter teaches that the separation not only did not happen, but *could* not happen: we remain as God created us, and our thoughts of hatred and attack had no effect on God's Love and our identity as God's children. Thus the Course urges us to change our minds from specialness to forgiveness, which is reflected in looking at our bodies differently. Learning to perceive the body objectively, without judgment, reveals to us our underlying thoughts of specialness, and this process of undoing is what the

Course means by forgiveness. It is therefore an essential part of Jesus' teachings in *A Course in Miracles* that his students learn to ask his (or the Holy Spirit's) help in providing a different perception of everything in the ego's world. As the Course says:

> Such is the Holy Spirit's kind perception of specialness; His use of what you made, to heal instead of harm (T-25.VI.4:1).

Thus, the body that the ego made as an instrument of hatred, murder, and fear, in the gentle perception of the Holy Spirit now becomes a classroom in which we learn the meaning of forgiveness. The basic issue, therefore, is whether we invite the ego's specialness to be our guide and interpreter regarding eating, or the Holy Spirit's forgiveness. The choice for the ego is an invitation to guilt and pain, while choosing the Holy Spirit invites love and joy. The ultimate choice therefore is not: to eat or not to eat. Rather the choice is with whom (or Whom) we *choose* to eat. And in that choice is found hell or Heaven:

> Perception is consistent with your choice, and …we choose between illusions and the truth, or pain and joy, or hell and Heaven (W-pI.130.10:3; W-pI.190.11:1).

Learning this single lesson is the goal of *A Course in Miracles*.

THE DIALOGUE

Betty: My whole relationship to food has been about more—always wanting more. My mother used to say, "Eat—you'll be hungry later." So that's what I've done all my life. I eat. I eat so I won't be hungry later.

Kenneth: And does it work?

Betty: No, I'm always hungry.

Kenneth: That means you always have to eat.

Betty: That's right. She also used to say, "We feed those we love." So, this is one of the places I come from. I always want to eat. No matter what goes on, a feeling or a thought, whatever, it always gets translated to: I want to eat.

Kenneth: Implied in what you are saying is that if you don't eat, if you don't *do* something, then something terrible is going to happen to you. And that's what gets us back to the basic teachings of the Course: if we keep quiet and we keep an empty space, then God is going to rush in and destroy us (W-pI.13.2:2). So we always have to fill up the emptiness. The ego first tells us that we are empty, and then it warns us that if God fills this emptiness we will be destroyed. Therefore we have to fill it ourselves. And so food is one of our favorite ways of doing that. The ego made

9

the body specifically so that it would be empty and lacking, always in need of something. The ego makes up all these wonderful things the world gives to fill us up. Food obviously is a big one—there are all kinds of other things too, but no matter what we choose, it's never enough because the whole system was made so that we would never have enough. That is, the system perpetuates itself continually because we eat and then we evacuate, and then we get hungry again—as your wise mother told you—and so we just keep eating and eating. The more we eat, the more we are shown how empty and lacking we are, which makes us more anxious, so we have to keep feeding the anxiety. And that is why it is an unending circle.

It's interesting, too, that on a level everyone shares, we always have to eat because our bodies are always getting hungry. We believe, for example, that if we don't eat we are going to die. What this refers to, of course, is the ego—if we don't keep feeding the ego system, then the ego is going to die. This is the thought that gets expressed in the body in terms of eating, because literally if we don't eat we *are* going to die. The system is set up that way. People who we identify as having food problems are manifesting an exaggerated sense of the same issue, just as people who we say are clinically insane or clinically paranoid, are simply manifesting in extreme forms what we all manifest. When the Course talks about the insanity of the ego, it is referring to the insanity we all have. And its extreme forms are found in the people we lock up. But the same thing holds with regard to food. Everyone has a food problem because we all believe we are bodies, and if we don't eat, something terrible will happen.

Susan: Well, that's really interesting to me because I always have a feeling which I've been associating—especially since I've been a student of the Course—with this terrible loneliness or yearning that I have. No matter what I'm doing, whom I'm with, or what I'm eating, I'm lonely. But in my search to fill this loneliness, it seems that food presents the most interesting opportunities for me. For example, I especially notice it when I'm in New York City: you can't walk ten feet without your senses being assaulted with all these magnificent displays of how this loneliness will be filled. There's the better ice cream and the better chocolate; it's just all over. I don't know how women who stay home all day are not obese, because in each half-hour program on television, there have to be thirty food commercials. And the food just looks wonderful, because of all the people who get this food looking as sumptuous as possible. So it always seemed to me that there was an unlimited supply, an infinite supply of very soothing, very interesting, exciting, loving ways of filling up the emptiness. I mean

11

if you eat pasta, it seems to me it's like replacing your mother: you know, it's warm, it's soothing, it's soft.

Kenneth: It fills you up.

Susan: Yes, it fills you up. If you eat chocolate, it's exciting—like sex. It seems to me there's a food for everything. So you really don't have to do anything but eat. Somehow when you put it in, that immediate feeling does displace that terrible loneliness.

Kenneth: Absolutely, that is its purpose. The ego made us to be lonely, and then it has the perfect remedy for it. Food works, and it works so effectively because on the basic physical level we do need food, otherwise we can't live. So that just feeds, pardon the pun, the whole system.

Judy: But it's just a temporary gratification, because the moment you're finished eating, you're looking for something else; and as Betty said, you are never ever satiated. I feel the same way, because I'm not filled up by food. It's just the immediate gratification, and then I'm looking for something else. And when you're not hungry but you're eating, you really start feeling guilty. I begin to wonder why I am doing this: I'm not even enjoying it anymore.

Kenneth: I think if you really pay attention to it, after a while you don't enjoy it. Something that people do is eat so much that they make themselves sick. At that point, then, it stops. I remember Bill Thetford telling me about a friend of his who was in London one time. He bought a pound of Black Magic chocolate, and ate the whole pound just like that. And he got so violently sick that he was out of shape for about a day or so. That's one way of solving the problem of anxiety, because otherwise you would just keep eating and eating. But if you really make yourself sick, then you're finished for a little while. That works perfectly, too.

Susan: It doesn't seem as if the Holy Spirit is as quick as the chocolate bar. Here I have this feeling—loneliness—and I have that candy bar, and I know the minute I put it in my mouth what is going to happen to me. Whereas I am not so sure where the Holy Spirit is at the moment I'm asking. One seems so immediate —notwithstanding the fact that I'm in torture immediately after I've eaten it; and it just seems as if we sort of have to wait for the No. 2 Bus before the Holy Spirit arrives, you know?

Kenneth: Again, the system is set up that way because the Holy Spirit has nothing to do with our bodies. He is in our minds, and if we believe we are bodies, then that is where the gratification has to come from. And, you're right—the Holy Spirit doesn't seem to work as quickly as chocolate does. It is also

13

true, just as you're saying, that you get the gratification, then afterwards you feel terrible. That's true of any special relationship: you are not aware that after the high goes, what is left is all the guilt. That is why you feel terrible. And then what do you do when you feel terrible? You've got to suffocate the guilt again and feed it; so then you keep eating—it's a cycle.

Betty: But with some people, this doesn't happen. Some people don't overeat. I'm fat, and some people aren't. I always need more, I want more, it's never enough for me. But for some people, when they finish eating, they finish. I'm considered obese by others, and I eat more than other people. Is that because I have more guilt? Is that it?

Kenneth: Are you saying it's not fair Betty?

Betty: Yes.

Susan: It sure isn't fair!

Kenneth: What you're saying certainly is true—I can understand that. But people choose their different forms; not all special relationships are the same in form. And so it's very possible the people whom you envy because they're thin and don't overeat, feel terribly guilty about something else—some kind of guilty secret, or secret shame. They would walk around envious of you because you don't have their form of neurosis and their specialness. So that food, overeating, is not the only form of specialness.

In one sense, since we all have to eat, that is something we share. But the excess of that is not for everybody, because people do different things. Why people do one or another is a whole different topic. There's no real answer for that, anyway. But the ego is always trying to say someone else has it better than I. I have it worse than someone else, just as you were joking before we started: "If you knew the deprivation I've had, then you'd understand why I overeat." Everybody feels that way—that I'm worse off than everybody else, and so there is a kind of insane competition to be more of a victim than other people, and that makes you special. But the temptation is always to compare ourselves to other people—either that we are better than others—or, what is really underneath that is the idea that I'm worse than others. And so perhaps one of the attractions of overeating is to keep yourself really miserable so that you are the greatest victim. Underneath that is the need to keep proving that I've been unfairly treated; and the way I do that is by continually demonstrating the problem I have, such as being overweight—whether I am actually physically overweight or just psychologically, i.e., I think I am. The more overweight I become—the more of a problem food becomes—the more I can point a guilty finger at someone, like my lousy parents, for example, who deprived me, and didn't give me the love, affection, and nourishment that I really wanted and felt I deserved. So each time I take a piece of chocolate, I'm really hammering another nail into their cross and saying, "You did this to me."

Susan: What you're getting into is what I've heard you say before, that behind every expression of guilt stands a person that you accuse, right? So if we are choosing to parade our guilt in the form of fat, then there's some person that that fat represents to us.

Kenneth: That's right.

Susan: But it's not important to find out who that person is, right?

Kenneth: You don't have to know who it is. All you have to know is that with each luscious spoonful of a hot fudge sundae, you are crucifying someone. So, the craving for the creamy, delicious, smooth, deep, dark chocolate symbolizes the hate for this person into whom you are driving a nail. That is exactly what it is.[3]

Susan: So the pleasure that I'm deriving out of whatever that food is, is in direct proportion to how I want to punish the person.

---

3. The reader may recall here the discussion in the Introduction of the metaphysical meaning of eating.

Kenneth: Yes, in one sense you can say that.

Susan: That makes sense to me: the degree to which I'm invested in the joy of this food is a key to the degree to which I really want to punish this person that I'm blaming for something.

Kenneth: That's the attraction—that's the pleasure.

Susan: Then, my gratefulness really becomes: if I didn't have this food, that for me is this ecstasy, I wouldn't ever be able to get at the depth of my need to forgive myself for accusing that person. Is that what you're saying?

Kenneth: Right. That is why dieting doesn't cure the problem, because the problem is not all the calories that you are consuming. The problem is all these murderous thoughts that are the content behind the form of the hot fudge sundae. Thus, if you give up the hot fudge sundae or the second helping, but the thoughts still stay there, you will just manifest them in another way.

That is why diets never work. You diet, you lose thirty or forty pounds, but the murderous thoughts are still there; and at some point, the urge just becomes overwhelming—you've got to nail the person to the cross again, and so you start eating.

Betty: If you are really willing to get to the murderous thoughts, then maybe one of the ways to do that is to stop overeating, so that you can get closer to them and deal with them a little more directly.

Kenneth: Yes. There's nothing wrong with dieting and limiting your food intake as long as you recognize that that is just an entree into the problem. I think that it is fine to have some kind of discipline, but if you don't do any changing of your mind, then nothing is going to happen. You may actually keep yourself thin, but you will dream of food all the time. Then you may sit down at a table or walk down a street where there are all these stores offering food, and you will be tempted all the time because the underlying thought has not changed. The temptation is not the food or the ice cream sundae: the temptation is murder. So, yes, on a practical level, I do think that it can be helpful to limit one's food and to have some kind of a diet. But if that is all that you do, you've done nothing.

Betty: What I am saying is that by limiting my food intake, the real issue will get uncovered. And then I can really deal with that. Then I can really see it as an issue of forgiveness, as an issue of blame.

Kenneth: Yes, forgiving your parents because they did not give you enough love when you were younger, or whomever else you're going to blame.

Susan: I don't buy that, I don't go for what you have just said. I keep challenging the Course by thinking that if it really works, I don't have to do anything to call upon the real connection. You can see I'm very resistant to going on a diet. I get very upset when I hear someone say, "If I go on a diet, and I'm a good little girl, and I restrict myself [which is the way I'm hearing what you've been saying I'm not] and do what the world tells me is the good little thing to do, and get my body a little nicer, then I'm going to get at those feelings and then I'm going to know who I want to murder." That really makes me go crazy because then I'm right back to saying that behavior is what makes me better or worse and I don't like that.

Kenneth: I think you are both right, because there is no formula. To say that I'll go on a diet, and then such and such will happen, could really work for certain people, and that becomes a means toward something else. It doesn't work for everyone. That would be lethal for someone like yourself. It wouldn't work; it would just bring up all your stuff, and all your resistance and opposition. Then you would just eat even more—to defy God again. But for some other people it could work. There's no right or wrong way of doing it. But what certainly is universal in this is that what ultimately has to change is the underlying thought. The means that we may choose to accomplish that would be different for each person, so for some people a diet really can be helpful and could work just the way you said, Betty. For you Susan, it wouldn't work at all.

Susan: When I'm on a diet, I find myself making a god of the diet, the way I made a god of the hot fudge sundae. The diet is my salvation or the hot fudge sundae is my salvation, and whether I'm eating the hot fudge sundae or not, I still want it. This leads me to the idea of the battleground. I find that my smart little ego is just keeping me in this terrible battle, and no matter what I do, it's wrong. I can't diet and be right; I can't not diet and be right. If I eat the hot fudge sundae, I hate myself; if I don't eat the hot fudge sundae, I hate myself—I've just built up this no win situation. And it's gotten worse since I've been a student of the Course, because now I can't even be right when I'm dieting. The years when I would diet and my body would be thin, I'd feel that at least I did something right. Now, I know that's not it either. So I just am creating this whole morass for myself, with no way out.

Kenneth: Right. And again, I think that regardless of the specific means a person uses, what you really want to do is try to understand what the eating is doing. You don't have to know who the specific person is that you are crucifying, but it is very helpful to realize that the problem is not the food, and that the food is just another form of murder.

Betty: You said a long time ago, if I can quote you loosely: "Eat without guilt and you'll get thin."

Kenneth: That was a good line.

Betty: That was terrific, Ken. And so, I decided to eat, whether it was with guilt or not with guilt.

Kenneth: That's not what I said.

Betty: Well, I figured I had to practice before I knew how to do it because I didn't even know what you were talking about. Every time you'd see me, you'd say, "You're getting thinner." Meanwhile, I'm watching the scale going up and up and up and up. I'm eating and eating and trying to do it without guilt. Of course, I didn't know how to do that and I never did. Of course I put on weight.

Kenneth: Then you blamed me.

Betty: Who else? You were perfect. You had even told me to do it. Then there was that idea of inviting the Holy Spirit to eat with me. So now I limit my food, and I don't eat hot fudge sundaes because I don't know how to eat a hot fudge sundae without guilt. But I have learned how to eat other food, lovely food, without guilt and with Spirit. And for the first time, after eating, it feels fine. I feel satisfied. But I have to eat seven hours later.

Kenneth: That gives you lots of practice though. I think that the reason it works is that it gets at the core problem we all have—the core separation problem that underlies feelings of deprivation, scarcity, and lack. Food is just one way of remedying that. The core problem is that we believe we have separated ourselves from God, which manifests itself in our every-day experience of separating ourselves from the Holy Spirit or from Jesus. And it is the guilt over that, that ferociously forces us to then find guilt in everyone else and kill them, which is a description of projection. Then, as you just said, each mouthful of food that we lusciously savor is another way of killing and crucifying someone.

This all comes from the feeling of lack inside us, because we have separated ourselves from the Love of God. When you bring the Love of God in with you to eat, you are undoing the root cause of the problem. And as you can experience that Love with you more and more, and feel a real Presence of the Holy Spirit or of Jesus with you, that's the beginning of the process of undoing the cause. The real reason for eating is not only to crucify someone out there, but to continually crucify God. Thus, if you are bringing the Presence of God in with you, then the whole purpose changes. In effect, you are really exacerbating what the conflict is, which also serves the helpful purpose of bringing it into awareness. That is its importance.

Betty: Of course I haven't learned how to eat chocolate without guilt...

Kenneth: All right; but if you start with a roast beef sandwich or mashed potatoes, or a bowl of corn flakes, or a cup of coffee, then that's something.

Susan: The process I went through started with inviting the Holy Spirit in when I was eating "bad foods," foods that I considered would make me fat. And I felt a lot better—I mean, I would have a transformational experience, my whole feeling would change and shift as I was eating when I would remember to invite the Holy Spirit in. But then I gained weight. Here I was, working my way through groups of food, literally, you know, first chocolate, then pancakes and waffles, and the desire for them disappeared once I ate enough of them, and I saw that the Holy Spirit wasn't going to let me feel guilty for all this stuff. But, there goes my body—and in a period of four months I gained ten pounds. Then of course I got very angry. So, what happened there? Why was I gaining weight?

Kenneth: What happened was that you forgot the purpose of the process. The purpose of the process was not to lose weight. The purpose of the process was for you to feel better about yourself and not feel guilty. What happened was that your ego was—as the ego always does—trying to sabotage you. The last thing in the world the ego wants you to do is to feel guiltless, and to feel loving and loved. So what it does, if it can't lick you, is join you. So it's not only the Holy Spirit Who is invited in for the pancakes and the hot fudge sundae, but the ego also. Thus, on the one hand, the Holy Spirit was allowing you not to feel so guilty because you felt a loving Presence within you that said, "It's okay, you're not sinful." But the ego was also there saying, "What do you mean you're not sinful; of course you're sinful. You're sinful because you're not feeling sinful. You broke one of the cardinal commandments that I gave you, and that is that thou shalt feel guilty when you have hot fudge sundaes, pancakes, and waffles." Therefore you said, "Oh my God, I'm having hot fudge sundaes, pancakes, and waffles —I must feel guilty." And so, voilà, you felt guilty. The upset that you felt when you gained ten pounds was not the cause of the ten pounds. That was just a smokescreen to give you some way of justifying why you felt guilty, and some way of proving that eating with the Holy Spirit doesn't work. It doesn't work because you had a hidden agenda: that eating with the Holy Spirit would mean that you would lose weight, so that when you *don't* lose weight, you can blame Him.

Susan: Right.

Kenneth: The weight is irrelevant. Eating with the Holy Spirit will result in loss of guilt: and that was working. And then your ego jumped in. It is the form/content confusion. To be guiltless is the content; losing or gaining weight is the form. What happened was that you forgot what the goal was. The Course says you set the goal first, and then you see the situation or the relationship as the means that serves the purpose of helping you attain that goal (T-17.VI.2-4). If the goal is to be guiltless, then you see eating the hot fudge sundaes and the pancakes as serving that purpose. Then it works beautifully. But if the goal is to lose weight, then the ego jumps right in and says you have failed.

Susan: I'm so afraid of this seductive god, which is saying to me: "Invite the Holy Spirit in, I love you; I care for you"; and I'm saying okay, and I'm doing it, and I'm getting fatter and fatter and fatter and fatter. That's how eventually I'm going to be really gotten. Oblivion for me is obesity. So this is a perfect scenario to work this whole scheme out to prove that God's really going to get me if I trust Him.

Kenneth: You are setting it up that way because part of you wants to prove that the Course doesn't work; this idea doesn't work; Jesus doesn't work; God doesn't work. That is the thought that has to change. So I think that if you went back to inviting Jesus or the

Holy Spirit in with you when you had all the sweets, and you felt better and said, "That's what I want, I want to feel better. I want to look in the mirror in the morning and not be concerned with what the scale says, because I know that the Love of God is within me, and I'm sinless and I've done nothing wrong"— if you could keep that goal always in mind, then you will also lose the weight. Because the putting on of the weight is part of your trap to prove that God is a liar. I don't think you did anything wrong except that you forgot what the purpose was. And your ego was saying the purpose was to lose weight.

Susan: So now, if I'm feeling too heavy to be able to follow that particular course, and I have now gone back to a sensible diet program, and I'm angry because I have to do that, then would the next step for me be to invite the Holy Spirit into the diet program?

Kenneth: Yes, I was just going to say that. That's right. You invite the Holy Spirit into the sensible diet program.

Susan: Because I can't handle all that weight trying to work it out the other way right now?

Kenneth: Right. And that's fine. Then you will realize that the Holy Spirit is with you whether you have a hot fudge sundae diet program, or you have a "sensible" diet program—it doesn't make any difference. That's an important lesson: that He loves you just as much when you're gorging yourself as when you're not. It makes no difference to Him.

Betty: Any goal of the body, whether it is that I want to be thin, I want to be thinner, or I'm only going to eat salad, is based on guilt. Therefore, it's not going to work.

Kenneth: Correct. It won't work. However, it *can* work, as a kind of temporary expedient, as you were saying earlier, as long as you are aware that what you are really doing is changing your mind and that the goal is to be guiltless. Salvation and the Love of God do not depend on my being twenty or thirty or forty pounds lighter or twenty or thirty or forty pounds heavier. It's totally irrelevant. The whole point, again, is that God loves me whether I have the hot fudge sundae or I don't. That's the lesson you want to learn.

Betty: There is something else now, in terms of behavior. We were talking briefly about addiction as a form of special relationships, but also as a very real manifestation of separation. And when I'm into food, I'm not joining with my brothers.

Kenneth: That is its purpose. Remember the whole purpose of overeating is to reinforce feelings of lack and separation. So when you are overeating, you are separating yourself from God; you are separating yourself from your parents if you are blaming them; you are separating yourself from people right now because you don't want to be with people when you eat, and you don't want to be with people when you're fat; etc., etc. But that's all that it is. It is just a way of proving that I was right and God was wrong, and separation, ugliness, and fat are the law: I'm hopeless and that will never change. But that's what it is: eating is a way of keeping you separate.

Judy: But it's also a way of joining. I feel very joined with people when sharing a meal with them. It's something that I very often look forward to.

Kenneth: At that point, though, the chances are that you won't overeat. If you are eating with someone and it's really an expression of love, of joining, then you are undoing the cause. It is the same thing as inviting the Holy Spirit in: the Course says that when you really join with someone, you are inviting the Holy Spirit in (T-17.V.2-3). So when joining with someone is the purpose of your eating, then there won't be any overeating, because the purpose has changed.

Susan: So, if during this process you invite the Holy Spirit in, you are beginning to undo the original purpose that you created to keep you separate. Then is the Holy Spirit going to lead you to your brothers?

Kenneth: Yes. He's not only going to lead you to your brothers; rather simply by inviting Him in, you *are* led to your brothers. It all works simultaneously.

Susan: What about hunger? Hunger is this great symbol to all of us, and I don't trust it. Some people say, when you're hungry, eat, and when you're not hungry, don't eat. I'm talking about the physical feeling of being hungry: I think that can be a set-up also. What is hunger?

Kenneth: Well, the ultimate hunger, of course, is the hunger after God. And if you redefine "hunger," which sounds more like a physical thing, to mean "yearning," it would be the same thing. What we all yearn for or hunger for is God. We know there's something missing. Everyone knows deep down there's something missing. Just as in that wonderful workbook lesson, "I will be still an instant and go home" (W-pI.182), which says at the beginning that everybody feels like an alien here, everybody feels that this world is not his or her home. Everybody.

In that very, very beautiful lesson, Jesus says, "No one here but knows whereof we speak." This world is not our home; we don't belong here; there's something missing. But then of course what people do, as the lesson also explains, is cover over those feelings, and join in specialness with others. We keep ourselves

29

busy and do all kinds of things: we try to make our bodies pretty, our apartments and homes pretty, the planet pretty; we want to make everything pretty because this is where we live. Of course, it never works. That is the yearning and the hunger that everyone has. What the ego always does is transfer that hunger and that yearning in the mind onto the body. That is another way of understanding why the body was made the way it was. The body is always getting hungry. I think for practical purposes we can set aside the normal hunger that the body will experience through the course of the day, just like the normal need for sleep. That is part of the ego system, but basically there are normal limits. We will rather talk about the *abnormal*, the ravenous hunger you feel even though you ate just an hour ago and your body doesn't need food—or you feel you have to sleep fourteen or fifteen hours a day, when your body doesn't need it. That is what we are talking about: the *excessive* hunger and need.

That is really the ego taking the sense of anxiety and lack, the feelings we all have of being orphans and homeless, and transferring them onto the body. Then it becomes that I have to deal with these physical feelings of being hungry and so on. The Course also explains that the body doesn't feel anything anyway. It is not the body that feels hunger; it is not the body that feels sexual, or that feels pain; it is the mind that then transfers its belief in lack to the body (T-19.IV-C.5:2-4;

T-28.VI.1-2). Then this becomes a very effective distraction device, a smokescreen, because we feel it is the body that has to be satiated; and so we go after whatever it is that will do it. But it never works because the underlying yearning is never fulfilled. That is why the system is "perfect," because it perpetuates itself continuously. That is why, just as you were saying Betty, it is never enough: I want more and more and more. It's the ego continually forcing us to focus on the body and then the world, which is going to provide the body with what it needs, so we never get to what we really need. Once again, if I could begin with the idea of inviting Jesus or the Holy Spirit in with me to eat, whether I eat sensibly or I gorge myself, I would begin to undo the thought system.

Susan: So, the behavior doesn't really matter.

Kenneth: Behavior doesn't matter—that's what traps you all the time with this. That is where you always get Jesus, you see. What he promises you is peace, love, happiness, and guiltlessness in your mind; and you say, "I don't want that, I want a thin body." You set the condition that way—like the story I tell of Helen and her non-negotiable demand of God.[4] You

---

4. *Absence from Felicity: The Story of Helen Schucman and Her Scribing of A COURSE IN MIRACLES*, 2nd edition, pp. 76-77.

tell Jesus this is non-negotiable: I want to lose twenty pounds.

Susan: Right.

Betty: And if you loved me you would let me.

Susan: Yes, you would *make* me.

Kenneth: That's right. And unconsciously you set it up that you *don't* lose the twenty pounds. See, you're the one who has chosen to gain the twenty pounds, not him. But you forget that and then blame him. It's an air-tight system. As the Course says: the ego system is foolproof—not Godproof, but foolproof (T-5. VI.10). It is air-tight within itself. Then you feel perfectly justified in giving him up, giving his Course up, giving diets up, giving everything up. Then you feel so terrible, you just eat even more, but what you have to do is realize that the whole thing is a set-up. You are setting it up so that it fails. The Course says the ego's maxim is "seek and do not find" (T-12.IV.1). That is what you are doing, because you may be doing what he is asking you to do in terms of inviting him in, but you are only doing part of it. You are doing the form of it, but not the content.

Susan: So, I'm doing the form of it. And, of course, I'm not doing it universally: I pick the foods, I pick the circumstances into which I invite the Holy Spirit.

So are you saying to invite the Holy Spirit into everything? Just keep generalizing it?

Kenneth: Yes, whether you are having a carrot or you are having a hot fudge sundae.

Susan: Keep inviting Him in whether I'm gaining weight or not. When I'm standing on the scale and I see the ten pounds, invite Him in for that experience —because I'd like a little company, as long as it doesn't make the scale go up!

Kenneth: The whole point that we had discussed another time about the hot fudge sundaes is that if you could have the hot fudge sundae with Jesus or the Holy Spirit with you, then there would not be any guilt.[5] That works, and it did work for you until your ego jumped in, sabotaged it, and said, "What do you mean it worked, I gained four pounds tonight!" But you lost four pounds of guilt, and *that* the ego doesn't tell you. What you really want to learn is that you are guiltless and that no matter what you believe you did to God or to Jesus, it has no effect on Their love for you. That is really what you want to learn. And your

---

5. The end of the teacher's manual (M-29.3:3) emphasizes how seeking the Holy Spirit's guidance puts an end to guilt. Once we choose to rejoin the Love of God instead of continuing to separate from it, we are able at last to correct the mistake made in the original instant, so that now love takes the place of terror.

ego is so afraid, that it says "No, no, no, I don't want to learn that, I want to lose weight."

Judy: So what happens is her goal keeps changing. She wants to be assured of the outcome, which is that she'll lose pounds on the scale, but the goal really is to be with God—you know, to align yourself with Holy Spirit so that your relationship with God deepens. But I see that there's always inconsistency there; we don't stay consistently in such company.

Kenneth: Because we are afraid of the goal. But what you want to do, as the Course says in many different places, is to keep your eyes, your mind always focused on the goal (see, e.g., T-17.VI; T-20.VII). The goal is to be guiltless, and to feel loving and peaceful. The inconsistency Judy is talking about is that we become afraid of that goal, because to the ego, to be without guilt is to be guilty. That is the problem. But then what you do is what we all do when it fails: rather than say, "Oh it failed because I got afraid of being guiltless," we say it failed because Jesus didn't come across, or he lied to me, or the Course is not true.

Susan: Or that the Course doesn't work.

Betty: Also, that we're not going to achieve salvation until we *all* do it. It's very hard for me. I may achieve some momentary loss of guilt, and so it doesn't matter. I don't care about the scale and the clothes I keep buying bigger, but the rest of the Sonship is going to look at me and go "ick."

Kenneth: Because you are holding them up?

Betty: No, because they're not guiltless either. And so they're going to see my fat.

Kenneth: Right, and they will attack it because they don't want to see it in themselves.

Betty: Then it's hard for me to walk around feeling okay when other people are not willing to be close to me because I'm fat.

Kenneth: But, if they are good students of *A Course in Miracles*, which is *their* responsibility not yours, they would recognize that when they get angry at Betty or get upset because Betty is overweight, it is really because of themselves. And so they should feel grateful for you, because you are then a screen that they could project their own inner fat onto.

Betty: Then I feel lonely for them, because there's a separation now between us.

Kenneth: There doesn't have to be. There doesn't have to be a separation in your mind. You know, you could see these people as your brothers and sisters. They may manifest their guilt in ways other than being overweight, and you manifest it in being overweight.

But you are still brothers and sisters because you share the same ego thought system. You also share the same yearning for God, but that is why that workbook lesson is so helpful. We all share the same yearning to go home, and we don't know how to. We don't know where it is. In fact, we feel that we've lost it and we're stuck here. It is like being in an ocean in a life raft. You know that this is not your home, but you don't know where home is, and you can't get there—you're just in a miserable life raft, in the middle of the ocean. If you realized that everybody is in a life raft and the way you get out is to join other life rafts, then you could all get home together.

The ego, then, is always going to keep you separate. Perceiving myself as separate from my brothers and sisters because I'm overweight and they are not, or as separate from my brothers and sisters because they are upset with the fact that I'm overweight, is the ego's way of looking at it. The other way of looking at it is that we are all upset, and we are all lost, and we all express our specialness in different ways. If you see it that way, you won't see your being overweight as an interference, or as a separating device. It then becomes a helpful device, a helpful way for you to realize that despite what you have made of your body, you still are not separate from anyone else, and despite all the food you are putting into your mouth, you still are not separate from anyone else or from

God. You have used it that way, but it does not have to be that way.

Judy: You know, I think that was one of the lessons in the Course that really hooked me. Yesterday the three of us were talking about causes and ways in which we join, and I said I was always a "cause" person. I always felt so separated from everyone in the world that I would join groups, or I would try to become involved in different things, thinking that someone had something I didn't have. And then when I would enter a new circle of friends or a new cause, I would find out that there was nothing there for me. I still had this empty feeling, and then I came upon that lesson, "I will be still an instant and go home." The lesson basically tells you this isn't your home—no one is at home here. There was just such a satisfying feeling because I knew then that I didn't have to search anymore for anything—that the search really was within. And again, it became establishing a deeper relationship with God, which I don't do all the time, but I know that's really where the goal is. I know that that's what the truth is for me. We spent a whole lot of time basically talking about that yesterday. We talked about the civil rights movement, and women's movements, and entering educational institutions, and getting degrees. I went that whole route. I had to accomplish it. I had to do it. Those were the goals I set. And then afterwards, I was still back where I started.

Kenneth: You're still hungry.

Judy: Still hungry. Yes. So I start binging on M & Ms.

Betty: Or starving. Here we've been talking about eating too much and overeating, and then there are people who starve themselves, who out of fear—in some cases, out of fear that they'll get fat—starve themselves and won't eat. They won't take in the nurturing and the love.

Kenneth: See, the ego gets us either way: it doesn't matter whether you become anorexic or just eat all the time. Ultimately, we should really think of food as an expression of cannibalism, which really is how the ego made the world and the body: there is something that I'm lacking and there is something outside me that I need, that will fill me up. Food literally does that. We do that all the time—psychologically in our relationships, but food is kind of a literal expression of that. And basically whatever it is that is outside us, we have to kill in order to eat. In other words, in order for a body to stay alive, whether it is a human body or any other so-called living organism, it has to kill something else and ingest it—whether you are killing a carrot, or you are killing a cow, or a fish, or whatever.

That activity holds the memory of what we did with God.[6] The ego does not exist if it does not stand on the death of God. So we have to kill God and eat Him, and that, of course, is what the Eucharist has been all about. Catholics at Mass ritualistically in the rite of communion eat the body of Jesus, so that his holiness, love, and life become their own, but at *his* expense. He is the sacrifice. It is the idea of having to kill. The teacher's manual says, in a sense, that the rule of the world is "kill or be killed" (M-17.7:11). This is the ego's world in our minds. Eating food, then, becomes a memory of that thought. Therefore it is no surprise, again, that almost everybody has ego issues surrounding food. The guilt is not because we have eaten something that was alive; the guilt is because we believe that we ate God, symbolically of course, because in the beginning there were no bodies. The ego tells us that we killed God. We stole from Him, and then upon His slain body we built our own kingdom.

Just to keep it simple, people can react to that guilt in two ways. One is to just keep going into the guilt: the more guilty I feel, the more I have to cover over all the pain. I just keep doing the very thing that makes me so guilty. People who are anorexic, or people who just don't eat very much because they are afraid of gaining

---

6. Recall again the Introduction, and our discussion of the Course's metaphysical principles.

an inch on their waistline or a pound on the scale, are going through what we call "reaction formation." They do the opposite: they make the "sin" of cannibalism real and then say, I don't do that, and I will prove to you, the world, and to God I don't do that because I'm thin. If I were fat, that's proof. I would be walking around giving witness to the fact that I am a living cannibal: I'm the one who has stolen from God. But if I could walk around thin all the time, then God can't point a finger at me; He'll point a finger at all those fat people. So I therefore magically hope that by not eating and by being thin, I could stave off that wrath of God and prove to Him I'm not the guilty one. The people who have to do that are just as fat as the people who are physically fat, because they are so guilty. It is the guilt that is the overweight, the obesity. Therefore, saying that I want to be thin is a way of saying I want to have the illusion of being innocent. It is always measured by the form, and that is why it never ever works.

Susan: So that's why we want to be thin, basically. To have the illusion of not being the guilty one. I didn't do this; somebody else did it.

Kenneth: Yes, and my being overweight then becomes a symbol: I have cannibalized; I have stolen something from outside me and put it inside me.

Susan: That is interesting because it goes back to something else you said, and I'd like to mention again: why people attack fat people, why society has made fat bad. You said something about our attacking it because we don't want to see it in ourselves. Could you bring that in here?

Kenneth: Basically, that would fit in nicely with what I just said. The core of the ego thought system is cannibalism. We cannibalize God, and when the Course talks about special relationships, even though it does not use the word "cannibalism," that is what it is talking about—that we wrested truth from itself (T-16.V.10-11). We believed we stole from God and stole from each other. And if that is the core of the ego system, that is where our guilt is. So our guilt is based upon our cannibalism, and then we live that out in form, in the body. So we made a body that literally has to cannibalize in order to survive. We thus look down upon the so-called primitives who are physical cannibals, eating human flesh. But that is what we all do. Whether it is human flesh, or animal flesh, or vegetable flesh, or whatever. That is what we do. And that is where the guilt is. The only way the ego can survive is to continually steal from God. This ego thought is then embodied in a body, which means the only way the ego body can live is to continually steal from other bodies. And since that is what food does, if I have

41

excess weight then that is the proof that I'm the guilty one. But we all feel that, whether one weighs 100, 200, or 500 pounds. I feel guilty because I stole from God. But if I am thin, I have the illusion I am innocent of that. And then I see *you* walking around at 250 pounds and I say, "Oh my, that's the proof, that's the proof that I've done it." And then I hate you. Part of me is trying to get away with it, and so I feel great that you are the one God is going to punish. But deep down I know that you are parading my sin in front of God, and at some point, God is going to find me out.

I think that is one of the reasons that so many people in the United States, vilified Nixon so much during his years—because he got caught. His mistake was not with the tapes and the breaking in and all that, because everybody steals and cheats—that is the ego world. But he got caught. And he got caught so bad that he had to leave the presidency. That is how bad that was. We hate him because, first, we see the sin in him. But the real hatred is that he exposed it for all of us. And that is why we hate all the rapists and all the criminals, and all the cheats, and all the financial big shots who get caught with insider trading, junk bonds, and everything else—because they are showing what is deep within everybody else. And I have tried so hard to keep it hidden. So I lose weight, keep myself thin, and am in such wonderful shape, looking so innocent. Then *you* walk along, bursting out of your clothes all over the place and the fat is just bulging—and my God, that's *me* that I'm seeing in you, and I hate you for it.

Susan: So tell me why in our American society our women are getting thinner? It's popular in the women's movement to blame it on the designers, because they're so greedy that they only want hangers for their clothes. But that is just really the surface. What is really going on? If you look at fashion today in 1990, you'll notice that you have to be far thinner in '90 than you had to be in '88 to wear the clothes that the designers are now showing.

Kenneth: It would follow the same pattern: the attempt to appear innocent. So being thin is a real value in our society. It wasn't always like that. There were cultures and time periods where being heavy was seen as a value. Look at the women in Reubens' paintings: they are all a little fleshy, and that was seen as something desirable.

Judy: During the Depression years, you know, it was a sign of prosperity.

Kenneth: It is helpful to see that it is all purely relative. In other words, it is how you look at it, which is the whole point of the Course, obviously. (See, e.g., T-21.V.1; T-22.III.3-8.) So while the forms change, the meaning is always the same. The meaning is that

I decide what form will prove that I'm innocent, and that I'm a good person. Presently, one of the favorite forms in our society is to be thin. So the attraction, the need, and the obsession with being thin is to say, "I'm innocent."

Susan: So because we are asking women to be thinner and thinner, our society is feeling more guilty, the guilt is sort of just piling up? Could we make that comparison?

Kenneth: I think there is a danger in suggesting that our society is getting guiltier—I'm not so sure that is the case. It is just that the form changes, and now the form in which I'm going to demonstrate my innocence is to be thin. During the Depression, again, the form in which my innocence would be manifest is in being heavy because being thin means I don't have any money, and ultimately it means God punished me. So then it becomes that I'm going to prove that God loves me because I'm fat or I look really healthy. That proves that I have money, it proves that God did not punish me and strip away from me everything that was mine—the way he did with Job, for example. That is why the story of Job is such a wonderful story of the ego's god, not the real God. God takes away. God gives you everything, and then He takes it away from you. And so, having all my money, and then losing it in 1929 proves that I am a failure. What I stole from God, He now stole back from me. He found me. It took Him a long time, but He found me, and He found where I hid all my jewels and everything I stole from Him. He took it from me, and now I don't have anything. Therefore, being thin proves that I am the guilty one and God punished me. Thus, during that period, the way I proved that God didn't punish me—He punished you—is that I'm fat. This means I'm prosperous, which means I didn't lose my money, which means God didn't steal it from me, which means I didn't steal it from Him, which means I'm off the hook. In our age now it is different, but it is the same idea.

Susan: Could you say then that what we are doing is just following this thought system to its natural conclusion? I mean, one year you're thin; then you have to be less guilty, so you want to be a little thinner the next year, maybe. We are never happy with food; we are also never going to be happy with our bodies. It's never going to be thin enough; it's never going to be voluptuous enough. That's why there is plastic surgery and all this other stuff.

Kenneth: Right. We will never have the perfect body. What everybody wants, whether you are a man or a woman, is to have the perfect body. And *you* decide what perfect is. So one time it is to be thin, another time it is to be fat. And it is the perfect body, because I want to deny what the body really is. The body is the symbol that I stole from God, that I am the greatest sinner in the world. The body, therefore, must be imperfect, which obviously it is because it's always breaking down. The body *must* be imperfect because it comes from an imperfect thought. So what I want to do is magically deny the imperfect thought, because that is where all my pain and misery and guilt come from. I deny this by saying, "But look, I'm perfect. I finally got my body to what it should be. It's the perfect size, the perfect width, the perfect weight, the perfect color, the perfect this, and so on. I've finally done it. I've proven that I'm innocent." And then the next day I wake up and something has broken down. I have a cold, or I gained half a pound, or I developed a pimple, or my hair is turning a little gray—and that means God found me out. My defense did not work and I am not perfect. That brings me right back to the imperfect thought, which is that I am guilty. And that is why it doesn't end.

Judy: Ken, in talking to Susan and Betty yesterday, I told them that most of my life I was thin, and that it is just recently that I have been having a problem with my weight, and I said I hated myself as much, if not more, when I was thinner. So I know the body isn't the answer. But yet there's something that just keeps me linked to the body. I kind of get into this obsessive behavior also, because I'm avoiding doing other work which is much more important than focusing on my body.

Kenneth: The body of course, is the great distraction, and that is why the ego made it. It is a wonderful distraction. We either think it is salvation or we think it is hell. And salvation really comes when we recognize the body doesn't make any difference. It is the purpose that we give to it. So you could be fat or see yourself as fat and not be bothered by it, and be grateful because it is a classroom in which you could learn that your body is not who you are. (See e.g., T-19.IV-B.10,14.)

Susan: That gets me back to another question that I've been saving, that you touched upon earlier—the idea that when guilt goes, fat goes. That's also a little shaky for me. It makes me a little nervous.

Kenneth: When guilt goes, the *obsession* with fat goes—that is what you want. You want to be without guilt, which obviously then means to be without the obsession with fat. But what you do is set it up in your mind so you are going to prove Jesus wrong.

Susan: So for me, holding on to the fat is going to mean that it doesn't work: Jesus isn't with me no matter how many times I ask him to join with me; it's not going to work for me.

Kenneth: Yes, you want it your way. Not just you, everybody. We want salvation our way. Basically we want to have our cake and eat it. We want to have God, but we want to have God in our own little box. And so you want to be without guilt, but you also want to be without fat—which means you are still making the body real, you are still making fat real, all of which means you're still caught.

Susan: So, as scary as this sounds, it could be part of my process of forgiving myself—since I have such an intense hatred of fat on my own body—to learn that I can be fat but peaceful, too. I hate to think of it.

Kenneth: Oh yes. I think it would be a wonderful lesson. You think you don't want that lesson because your fat is such a problem. The real reason you don't want that lesson is that you will really feel peaceful— that is what you are afraid of. There is that wonderful section in the text, "The Fear of Redemption," where Jesus says that our real fear is not of crucifixion: our terror is of redemption (T-13.III.1-5). That is what you are really afraid of: if you let go of your obsession with fat, you'll be happy. And so to protect yourself against being happy, you keep getting crazy about food and your body. It is set up that you will never feel happy, which is just what your ego wants.

Betty: You were talking about the perfect body. I loved Susan's image of when you die and finally get to see God, there He is…corpulent, billowing in layers of fat. Oh my God, I could have been fat all this time—and happy. I wanted to be thin, and fat was what it was all about!

Kenneth: And happy. Think of all the statues of the fat Buddha. We make God in our own image, obviously, but the idea would be that you could be just as happy in this world and be overweight, as underweight or thin.

Betty: We've been talking about all of our dissatisfactions with the body, I mean, whether it's curly hair, or straight hair, or long hair, or short hair, or makeup or no makeup, or sneakers, or whatever.

Kenneth: It's all the same. We identify ourselves with our bodies, and in one sense the ego's goal is the same as the Holy Spirit's, but it ends up totally different. The Holy Spirit's goal, obviously, is for us to be without guilt. That is what the ego tells us its goal is for us as well. It tells us that we will be without guilt. Its underlying goal, its true goal, of course, is to keep us guilty. But it tells us its goal is to have us be guiltless, and so it takes the guilt in our minds and projects it onto the body. Then we say the body is the problem—now we have something tangible. What really happens is that the guilt in the mind stays there. So now the guilt is in the body, and the ego says, "Well, now I'm going to make your body perfect. And then you will be guilt-less and you will feel wonderful." One of the prevalent forms of this—and that's why we are here today—is the belief that what will keep me guiltless and what will keep me feeling good is to be thin. And so I listen to my ego's plan for salvation, and that is what it is: it translates into, "I will be thin." Then I struggle and struggle to become thin. The ego is always preoccupied with the body. The guilt in my mind rests very safely and happily, and never gets touched.

Susan: You know, it's so hard to see that we project onto our bodies the same way we project onto people. If I get upset at something Betty does, if I accuse Betty of being mean and I get really upset, I can see that I have projected onto Betty a self-accusation of being mean, and the person I have to forgive is myself. But when we do that with our bodies, since we identify ourselves as only being our bodies, it is very difficult to understand that I'm projecting onto my body. When I am accusing my body of being unlovable because I'm fat, it's just another projection as though I were doing it to Betty.

Kenneth: It is no different, because your body is as much outside your mind as Betty's body is outside your mind. It makes no difference.

Susan: That's harder to see for me.

Kenneth: Yes, but that's the way out of it for you: to realize that you are setting it up so that you will always feel guilty, and then blame somebody else. Ultimately, you will blame God for it. In a sense, you have written the rules and you hold all the cards, because you could control whether your body gains weight or not. If your purpose is to prove that God is a liar and that you are a failure, you could do that because you have set up the rules so that you will gain weight, and therefore you will always gain weight.

Susan: Will you talk about that? I've heard you say before that you don't gain weight from the calories in food; you gain weight from a decision you've made.

Kenneth: Right—just as smoking doesn't give you cancer: guilt gives you cancer. A decision in your mind to be guilty is what gives you the cancer. It is the same thing. You gain weight because your mind gives your body an instruction that says, "Gain weight because that is what will prove that you are ugly, worthless, sinful, and separate." As Betty keeps saying, food keeps you separate. It certainly keeps you separate from your real Self. It keeps you separate

51

from the Love of God in you. It keeps you separate from Jesus because you blame him. And it keeps you separate from other people because you are so ashamed of yourself. And on and on it goes. Gaining weight, then, comes from a wish to be separate—a wish to blame yourself, a wish to be guilty. It was the mind, the ego mind, that made up the body and the laws of the body. Now, one of the laws of the body is that if you eat five hot fudge sundaes, you are going to gain weight. You will get a little sick, too, but you will gain weight. That is what makes you gain weight. It is the same idea as saying that if I lift up this watch and drop it, it will fall to the ground because of the law of gravity. It didn't drop because of the law of gravity—there *is* no law of gravity.[7] The mind made up a law of gravity that says if I hold the watch and drop it, it is going to fall. But if my mind changed that law, if my mind changed what it wanted, then I would let go of this and it would hang in the air. It drops not because of the law of gravity; it drops because we made up the law of gravity and placed ourselves under its bondage.

----

7. I am speaking metaphysically. In reality, there is no law of gravity since there is no material universe. The world is simply a thought of separation in our minds; a thought that is deeply buried in our unconscious minds, and is shared by almost everyone.

Susan: That is why some people can eat inordinate amounts of food and not gain weight, and others eat and gain weight.

Kenneth: That's right—because that is how our minds set it up. Then those of us who are overweight feel guilty and feel terrible because we eat and we gain weight, and there's another person who eats and gains nothing. We don't accept responsibility for having made ourselves that way. I could realize though, that I made myself that way so that I could feel guilty about what I'm doing. So what I want to change is not what my body looks like; what I want to change is how my mind thinks (T-21.in.1). It is all in my mind: I gain weight when I have hot fudge sundaes because I programmed myself like that.

Susan: That's the bad food to me.

Kenneth: Yes, that is a bad food for you, because you have set up the world in terms of good food and bad food. What you have really done is project onto the world and onto food a split that is in your mind. There is a good you and a bad you; and the ultimate split is the two warring factions in the mind: the ego and the Holy Spirit. My ego is good and the Holy Spirit is bad. But everything is seen in terms of dichotomy and opposites. This is the split you put onto the world: there is good food and bad food. Then there is good Susan and bad Susan. There is good Susan when she eats the good food, and bad Susan when she eats the bad food.

Betty: Now current addictions theory views compulsive overeating as an avoidance of feelings. They talk all about feelings now. So you're talking about feelings of guilt; they talk about feelings of pain and loss. So this is all the same.

Kenneth: Yes, it is basically all the same. I think that the Course takes it one step further. But basically, it is all the same. Eating is a way of stuffing feelings. I'm anxious, and so I will stuff it. I will just stuff layers of food, or layers of alcohol, or layers of drugs, or whatever the addiction is—money, possessions, or sex. Whatever the obsession is, it is going to cover over the anxiety and the pain. So in that sense it would be similar.

Betty: Can we talk about the anxiety and the pain? I said before that if you stop eating, then you'll really get in touch with some of that guilt and then look at that, and it'll free you to really deal with that with the Holy Spirit. But now let's just talk in these terms: I'm doing this to relieve anxiety, and to not have to feel the pain, and to not have to.... So what are feelings?

Kenneth: One of the things that the ego has done is to make things very, very complicated. There is only one feeling in the ego mind, and that is guilt—or we could use the word "fear." You could talk about feelings of anxiety, feelings of panic, feelings of inadequacy, feelings of insecurity, etc., etc.; but they all basically come from the same thing. That is what we don't want to look at. What the ego does is take the feeling of guilt or the belief in guilt which is in the mind, transfer it onto the body, and then we have certain feelings in the body, whether it is the physical body or the psychological body (one's personality). Then that is what we have to take care of (T-18.VI.2-6; T-18.IX.4-5).

See, the ego always gets us further and further away from what the problem is. The problem ultimately is the guilt in my mind: I feel unworthy of God's Love, because I believe I've separated from Him. I transfer that onto my body, and then I feel bad, for example, because I was deprived as a child. That emotional feeling of being deprived as a child has nothing to do with my parents; it ultimately has to do with what I have done with God. This gets translated directly into a bodily feeling of emptiness: there is a lack in me and I have to fill it up with food. So, food then takes on the symbolic meaning of love, which obviously it does. Thus, I feel deprived of love, lacking in love, so I have to fill my body with love, which is food. I don't want to deal with the feeling of pain that my parents didn't love me, so then I just fill up with the food. Again, as

I said at the beginning, each time I take a morsel of food, I'm crucifying my parents and saying, "If you had loved me and had been nourishing as you were supposed to, then I wouldn't have to gorge myself and look so ugly and fat—it's all your fault." In that sense, what people are talking about these days is true: food is a defense. It is a defense against looking at myself.

Now, where the Course would differ is in saying what food is a defense against: it is not what happened forty years ago when my parents didn't give me enough love. It is a defense against a decision I am making right now. But that it is a defense, is true— overeating is a defense, just as undereating is a defense. It is a way to keep us from the feelings or thoughts that are underneath it. Again, the Course redefines what those thoughts are.

Betty: You just equated guilt and fear. Could you just talk about that for a minute?

Kenneth: Basically as you know, I talk about sin, guilt, and fear. We feel sinful because we have separated from God. We feel guilty because of what we have done, and then we are afraid of God's punishment (see p. 2 above). We talk about them as if they were discrete entities. That is an easy way to talk about them because our minds are oriented to think in linear terms. In reality, they are all the same. They are a constellation of the same thought. The Course will very often go back and forth between sin and guilt, or guilt and fear. And so that is really what I did. The section "The Two Emotions" says of fear and love: "one you made and one was given you" (T-13.V.10). So God gave us love and we substituted fear for it. But you can just as easily use the word "guilt." And basically it is not an emotion, even though that section talks about emotions. Love certainly is not an emotion. The Love of God is not an emotion as we know it. And fear really is a thought. We experience it as an emotion because thoughts are translated into bodily experiences for us by the ego. So I feel fear and I know what fear is, and we talk about fear as an emotion. But ultimately it is a thought. It is the thought of being separate from God and the thought of being punished. Then I feel my adrenaline race and I feel very anxious, and I feel I have to starve the feeling or suffocate the feeling—escape from it, etc. But it is basically only thought.

Susan: In terms of what Betty just said, there is no magic either. While there's nothing wrong with it, there's no magic in getting to those feelings. In other words, what Betty is saying is that the prevailing thought in addictions theory is that you're stuffing down the feelings, and the best thing to do is to stop stuffing them down: deal with the feelings. But that's a trap, too. There's no magic anywhere. I mean, it doesn't really matter. It might work for you; it might be helpful, but that is not the sure way to do it.

Kenneth: That's right.

Susan: Since all those feelings are represented in everything we do anyway, and it's only all guilt, then the only thing that "works" is inviting in the Holy Spirit. Is that what you're saying?

Kenneth: Yes, absolutely right. That is the bottom line: recognizing that all of our problems come from guilt, and that guilt stems from the belief in being separate from God. That is the problem. The Course over and over says how simple it is—there is one problem, one solution. The problem is separation, and the solution is the Holy Spirit (W-pI.79,80). What we do is take that guilt which is abstract, and which is a thought buried deep in our minds, and we project it onto the body. The form that the guilt takes—which we are discussing specifically here—is the form of being overweight and overeating. I feel guilty, and then I feel fat and I feel ugly. And that proves to me how unworthy and how guilty I am. If I could always be clear that the problem is not the number on the scale in the morning, but rather that I feel separate from God, and if I would keep maintaining that, then the solution is not to lower the number on the scale, but to invite the Holy Spirit to look at the problem with me. That is always the bottom line. For example, I can then invite the Holy Spirit to have the hot fudge sundae with me, and then feel okay about it and okay about myself as well. I would be feeling good about myself because of the Loving Presence I have called into my awareness. That is what I want. Then the Holy Spirit helps me look at my obsession with food and my ravenous hunger, and tells me that it is not a big deal: "What you are really hungry for is Me, and I am right here with you. I am what you want, not the hot fudge sundae. But until you can accept Me and accept My Love, I will join with you in eating the hot fudge sundae."

Helen used to have Jesus go with her when she shopped. She was obsessed with shopping. She was also obsessed with eating, but she solved that problem by just being very strict with herself. Helen always felt that Jesus was going with her and telling her where to shop. It was comforting to her to feel that he was not condemning her or judging her. And he never once told her not to shop, until many, many years later.[8]

One afternoon, I remember we left the Medical Center to go shopping. We used to go along Fifth Avenue to Lord & Taylor and Altmans, and then we

---

8. *Absence from Felicity*, 2nd edition, pp. 229-30, 426-27.

would go to all the shoe stores on 34th Street. That was our ritual. That day Helen said, "*He* told me" (she didn't always say "Jesus"), "He told me I shouldn't do this anymore—that it was no longer good for me."[9] Now this was after years and years and years. From that point on we never went shopping—certainly not that ravenous, obsessional kind of shopping. But it took a long, long time. And her experience, which was really important for her, was that Jesus did not condemn her because she was using her clothes and her shopping to avoid him. It was obvious that that was what she was doing. We would spend several hours on a Saturday going around to all these stores never finding anything, only to—at the end of the day—spend a half hour praying together with Jesus. It was almost as if she had to do all this stuff first, so then she could spend twenty minutes or a half hour with him. The whole day was meant, in one sense, as a distraction from him, and at the same time it was her way of compromising and saying, "Well I'll give you a little time later, but you've got to give me several hours."

Susan: We're doing the same thing with food.

Kenneth: Exactly.

---

9. By this Jesus meant that Helen was able now to let go of her defense against him.

Susan: We're going to all the restaurants, eating all the foods, having all the meals and then maybe....

Kenneth: Then we say to Jesus, "If I've gained any weight, then the hell with you; I'm not going to let you in anyway." The idea is to bring him with you, whether "him" is Jesus or the Holy Spirit or God—whatever term you are going to use. That enables you not to feel so guilty. And that is the purpose. The idea is always to keep in mind what the purpose is—and it is not that you be thin. The purpose is that you feel good about yourself. But if feeling good about yourself is wedded to the size of your waistline, then you're finished. On the other hand, if feeling good about yourself is wedded to the Holy Spirit's Presence in your mind, then the ending will be a happy one. That Presence is constant, and that never changes. That is the idea. That is the value of letting Jesus in with you, whether you are eating "good" food or "bad" food. That is really what you have to learn: that he will be with you when you have salads, and he will be with you when you have hot fudge sundaes. That is his way of teaching you it doesn't make any difference: "My love for you does not depend on whether you are good or bad."

Susan: It's like one of the first workbook lessons which says to look around the room but don't exclude anything (W-pI.1.3; W-pI.2.2). You're saying the same thing.

Kenneth: The exact same thing.

Susan: It just sounds so simple. Not easy. But now, with every step of the way no matter what it is, no matter what you're doing, no matter what judgment you made about it, invite the Holy Spirit in. Period. End of the story.

Kenneth: That is what you do. Then look with Him, step back and watch with Him while you gorge yourself, or while you eat a salad which only has 150 calories in it. Stand back and watch with Him while you do this. That is what helps you begin to put distance between yourself and the food, and change the purpose of the food. Then food becomes holy instead of a symbol of your unholiness, your guilt, your sinfulness, and your failure. It becomes a symbol telling you that this is the way that Jesus or the Holy Spirit is going to teach you that He loves you (W-pII.5.4; T-8.VII.3).

Susan: Even when you're gorging yourself.

Kenneth: Even when you're gorging yourself. It doesn't make any difference.

Susan: Because you're doing it with the Holy Spirit.

Betty: The Holy Spirit uses everything. With the Holy Spirit everything can be a lesson for forgiveness.

Kenneth: Right. That purpose of forgiveness then becomes the importance of everything in the world. Actually you should think of this very literally in terms of food. There's a line in the Course that says the Holy Spirit never takes your special relationships away from you; He transforms them (T-17.IV.2; T-18.II.6). He will never take the hot fudge sundae away from you—He will transform its meaning. And when the meaning changes, in time the hunger for it will change. The hunger for the hot fudge sundae is to punish yourself, and to keep God away and to keep your true Self away from you—that is the "true" meaning of it. That is the hunger for it. When you bring God with you, then the whole thing has changed and that is when the yearning will go. But you can't sabotage this by then jumping on a scale afterwards.

Susan: But if you do get on the scale, you invite the Holy Spirit again. And, also, when you get mad because the numbers went up, you invite the Holy Spirit again, and no matter where your ego goes, you tag along with the Holy Spirit right there. So you just keep doing that.

Kenneth: That's the answer.

Susan: And so the *only* faith that's asked here, is the faith that if you do this with the Holy Spirit, or the Love of God, or the memory of God, or whatever, that eventually you're going to feel better.

Kenneth: That's right. And then you stop: I will feel better; not I will be thin—I will *feel* better.

Susan: So your focus then has to be with feeling better, not with anything else.

Kenneth: Yes, that is the goal. As we have already said, you set the goal first. There is a section in the text called "Setting the Goal," which explains this nicely (T-17.VI). If the goal is to be thin, then that is what you may achieve, but you're not going to find peace. If my goal is to be guiltless, to feel good about myself and to feel God's Love within me, then I will see eating the hot fudge sundae as the means to achieve that end. If I see the goal as losing weight, then I will see that the goal of not eating the hot fudge sundae is to lose weight, and I will probably fail, because it was set up to fail. But if I see eating the hot fudge sundae as the means to achieve the goal of being guiltless, and I eat the hot fudge sundae with Jesus next to me and I feel guiltless, then I've won, and Jesus has won too. See, *your* way is that one is going to win and one is going to lose. You are going to be right, and you are going to prove that he is wrong. If the goal, however, is that we are both right, and that we are both right because I want to be guiltless, and that is the purpose of my eating—whether it is a hot fudge sundae or a carrot—then I will eat, feel guiltless, and say, "It does work."

Susan: So that would also be the purpose of my fat. The purpose of my fat, because I've followed you, I've gone through all the steps, and I'm eating hot fudge sundaes and eating whatever those foods are, and I'm fat—the purpose of the fat would be to prove that I'm guiltless: to use the fat as that transformational lesson that God loves me.

Kenneth: Right. And the fat then becomes your friend. There is a wonderful line in the teacher's manual that says, "Do not despair, then, because of limitations [it is referring to the limitations of the body]. It is your function to escape from them, but not to be without them" (M-26.4:1-2). We can translate that now in terms of fat: "Do not despair, then, because of the limitations of your fat. It is your function to escape from it, but not to be without the fat." In other words, it is your function to escape from the guilt and the anger, the hopelessness, despair, inadequacy, and self-hatred that you have associated with the fat; but your function is not to be without it. It does not mean you won't be without it some day, but that is not the function. The function is to escape from the guilt or the interpretation you placed on the fat. If that is what the lesson is, then you will be so grateful to the fat because you learned a lesson that would have taken thousands and thousands and thousands of years to learn within the illusion of time—and that is that you are guiltless.

Susan: And so the intensity of my hatred of the fat will be the intensity of my healing, the depth of my healing once I really learn that lesson—I'm now healed to that degree. Is that what you're saying?

Kenneth: That is what I am saying.

Susan: I never thought I'd be happy to be fat. Wow.

Betty: Wait, it hasn't happened yet.

Kenneth: Let me read something as a way of closing. It is from the workbook, the section that answers the question, "What is the Body?" I will just read part of it. We can translate it into the terms of what we have done with the topic of being overweight: we have made the body to attack and keep God away, and we have made fat as a way of proving that we have succeeded. Our body thus has become a terrible symbol of our sin against God. The body does not disappear nor does the overweight disappear; but the function changes, and by changing that function, or the purpose of the body, the body then becomes holy. Basically what we have done with the body is that we

66

have used it to identify with our guilt and fear, as a defense against what we really want to identify with, which is the Love of God or the Love of Christ that we are. What we identify with is what will prove to us who we are. The section ends with the idea that we should identify with love and not with the body. And so it is possible, then, to use the body as a means of reminding ourselves that we really are love, and bringing the Holy Spirit or Jesus in with us is what does that. Again, it is all a question of what the body is for. So we will close with my reading portions of this section from the workbook:

> The body is a fence the Son of God imagines he has built, to separate parts of his Self from other parts. It is within this fence he thinks he lives, to die as it decays and crumbles. For within this fence he thinks that he is safe from love. Identifying with his safety, he regards himself as what his safety is. How else could he be certain he remains within the body, keeping love outside?...
>
> The body is a dream. Like other dreams it sometimes seems to picture happiness, but can quite suddenly revert to fear, where every dream is born. For only love creates in truth, and truth can never fear. Made to be fearful, must the body serve the purpose given it. But we can change the purpose that the body will obey by changing what we think that it is for.

The body is the means by which God's Son returns to sanity. Though it was made to fence him into hell without escape, yet has the goal of Heaven been exchanged for the pursuit of hell. The Son of God extends his hand to reach his brother, and to help him walk along the road with him. Now is the body holy. Now it serves to heal the mind that it was made to kill.

You will identify with what you think will make you safe. Whatever it may be, you will believe that it is one with you. Your safety lies in truth, and not in lies. Love is your safety. Fear does not exist. Identify with love, and you are safe. Identify with love, and you are home. Identify with love, and find your Self. (W-pII.5.1,3-5)

text

workbook for students

manual for teachers

Psychotherapy: Purpose, Process and Practice

Foundation for A COURSE IN MIRACLES®

Kenneth Wapnick received his Ph.D. in Clinical Psychology in 1968 from Adelphi University. He was a close friend and associate of Helen Schucman and William Thetford, the two people whose joining together was the immediate stimulus for the scribing of A COURSE IN MIRACLES. Kenneth has been involved with A COURSE IN MIRACLES since 1973, writing, teaching, and integrating its principles with his practice of psychotherapy. He is on the Executive Board of the Foundation for Inner Peace, publishers of A COURSE IN MIRACLES.

In 1983, with his wife Gloria, he began the Foundation for A COURSE IN MIRACLES, and in 1984 this evolved into a Teaching and Healing Center in Crompond, New York, which was quickly outgrown. In 1988 they opened the Academy and Retreat Center in upstate New York. In 1995 they began the Institute for Teaching Inner Peace through A COURSE IN MIRACLES, an educational corporation chartered by the New York State Board of Regents. In 2001 the Foundation moved to Temecula, California, and shifted its emphasis to electronic teaching. The Foundation publishes a quarterly newsletter, "The Lighthouse," which is available free of charge. The following is Kenneth and Gloria's vision of the Foundation.

In our early years of studying A Course in Miracles, as well as teaching and applying its principles in our respective professions of psychotherapy, and teaching and school administration, it seemed evident that this was not the simplest of thought systems to understand. This was so not only in the intellectual grasp of its teachings, but perhaps more importantly in the application of these teachings to our personal lives. Thus, it appeared to us from the beginning that the Course lent itself to teaching, parallel to the ongoing teachings of the Holy Spirit in the daily opportunities within our relationships, which are discussed in the early pages of the manual for teachers.

One day several years ago while Helen Schucman and I (Kenneth) were discussing these ideas, she shared a vision that she had had of a teaching center as a white temple with a gold cross atop it. Although it was clear that this image was symbolic, we understood it to be representative of what the teaching center was to be: a place where the person of Jesus and his message in *A Course in Miracles* would be manifest. We have sometimes seen an image of a lighthouse shining its light into the sea, calling to it those passers-by who sought it. For us, this light is the Course's teaching of forgiveness, which we would hope to share with those who are drawn to the Foundation's form of teaching and its vision of *A Course in Miracles*.

This vision entails the belief that Jesus gave the Course at this particular time in this particular form for several reasons. These include:

1) the necessity of healing the mind of its belief that attack is salvation; this is accomplished through forgiveness, the undoing of our belief in the reality of separation and guilt.

2) emphasizing the importance of Jesus and/or the Holy Spirit as our loving and gentle Teacher, and developing a personal relationship with this Teacher.

3) correcting the errors of Christianity, particularly where it has emphasized suffering, sacrifice, separation, and sacrament as being inherent in God's plan for salvation.

Our thinking has always been inspired by Plato (and his mentor Socrates), both the man and his teachings. Plato's Academy was a place where serious and thoughtful people came to study his philosophy in an atmosphere conducive to their learning, and then returned to their professions to implement what they were taught by the great philosopher. Thus, by integrating abstract philosophical ideals with experience, Plato's school seemed to be the perfect model for the teaching center that we directed for so many years.

We therefore see the Foundation's principal purpose as being to help students of *A Course in Miracles* deepen their understanding of its thought system, conceptually and experientially, so that they may be more effective instruments of Jesus' teaching in their own lives. Since teaching forgiveness without experiencing it is empty, one of the Foundation's specific goals is to help facilitate the process whereby people may be better able to know that their own sins are forgiven and that they are truly loved by God. Thus is the Holy Spirit able to extend His Love through them to others.

Responding in part to the "electronic revolution," we have taken the Foundation's next step in our move to Temecula, California. With this move to a non-residential setting we are shifting our focus, though not exclusively, from totally live presentations to electronic and digital forms of teaching in order to maximize the benefits of the burgeoning field of electronic media communication. This will allow us to increase our teaching outreach, the *content* of which will remain the same, allowing its *form* to adapt to the 21st century.

Related Material on
A Course in Miracles

By Kenneth Wapnick, Ph.D.

Books

(For a complete list and full descriptions of our books and audio and video publications, please see our Web site at www.facim.org, or call or write for our free catalog.)

Christian Psychology in *A Course in Miracles*. Second edition, enlarged.
ISBN 978-0-933291-14-0 • #B-1 • Paperback • 90 pages • $5.

Translation available in Spanish.

**A Talk Given on *A Course in Miracles*:
An Introduction.** Seventh edition.
ISBN 978-0-933291-16-4 • #B-3 • Paperback • 131 pages • $6.

Translations available in Afrikaans, Danish, Dutch, Finnish, French, German, Italian, Portuguese, Romanian, Slovene, and Spanish.

Glossary-Index for *A Course in Miracles*. Sixth edition, revised and enlarged.
ISBN 978-0-933291-03-4 • #B-4 • Paperback • 228 pages • $8.

Translations available in German and Spanish.

Forgiveness and Jesus: The Meeting Place of *A Course in Miracles* and Christianity. Sixth edition.
ISBN 978-0-933291-13-3 • #B-5 • Paperback • 399 pages • $16.

Translations available in German and Spanish.

The Fifty Miracle Principles of *A Course in Miracles*. Fifth edition.
ISBN 978-0-933291-15-7 • #B-6 • Paperback • 107 pages • $8.

Translations available in German and Spanish.

Awaken from the Dream. Third edition. Gloria and Kenneth Wapnick.
ISBN 978-0-933291-04-1 • #B-7 • Paperback • 97 pages • $10.

Translations available in German and Spanish.

Love Does Not Condemn: The World, the Flesh, and the Devil According to Platonism, Christianity, Gnosticism, and *A Course in Miracles*.
ISBN 978-0-933291-07-2 • #B-9 • Hardcover • 614 pages • $25.

A Vast Illusion: Time According to *A Course in Miracles*. Third edition.
ISBN 978-0-933291-09-6 • #B-10 • Paperback • 302 pages • $14.

Translation available in German.

Absence from Felicity: The Story of Helen Schucman and Her Scribing of *A Course in Miracles*. Second edition.
ISBN 978-0-933291-08-9 • #B-11 • Paperback • 498 pages • $17.

Translations available in Danish, German, and Spanish.

Overeating: A Dialogue. An Application of the Principles of *A Course in Miracles*. Second edition.
ISBN 978-0-933291-11-9 • #B-12 • Paperback • 70 pages • $5.

A Course in Miracles **and Christianity: A Dialogue.**
Kenneth Wapnick and W. Norris Clarke, S.J.
ISBN 978-0-933291-18-8 • #B-13 • Paperback • 110 pages • $7.

Translations available in German and Spanish.

The Most Commonly Asked Questions About *A Course in Miracles*. Second edition. Gloria and Kenneth Wapnick.
ISBN 978-0-933291-21-8 • #B-14 • Paperback • 113 pages • $8.

Translations available in Danish, Dutch, German, and Spanish.

The Message of *A Course in Miracles*. **Volume One: All Are Called. Volume Two: Few Choose to Listen.**
Two Volumes: 619 pages.
ISBN 978-0-933291-25-6 • #B-15 • Paperback • $22 (set).

Translations available in German and Spanish.

The Journey Home: "The Obstacles to Peace" in *A Course in Miracles*.
ISBN 978-0-933291-24-9 • #B-16 • Paperback • 510 pages • $16.95.

Ending Our Resistance to Love: The Practice of *A Course in Miracles*.
ISBN 978-1-59142-132-0 • #B-17 • Paperback • 94 pages • $7.

Translations available in Dutch, German, and Spanish.

"What It Says": From the Preface of *A Course in Miracles*.
ISBN 978-1-59142-208-2 • #B-25 • Paperback • 78 pages • $8.

The Arch of Forgiveness.
ISBN 978-1-59142-210-5 • #B-27 • Paperback • 103 pages • $7.

Ordering Information

Additional copies of this book may be ordered
at our Web site: www.facim.org, where a complete list
of our publications may be found.

Orders may also be placed by calling or writing our office at:
Foundation for A COURSE IN MIRACLES®
Dept. B
41397 Buecking Drive
Temecula, CA 92590
(951) 296-6261 • FAX (951) 296-5455

A Course in Miracles and other scribed material
may be ordered from:

Foundation for Inner Peace
P.O. Box 598
Mill Valley, CA 94942
(415) 388-2060

A Course in Miracles, Second Edition, Complete:
Hardcover - 6" x 9": $35
Softcover - 6" x 9": $30
Paperback - 5" x 8": $20

Psychotherapy: Purpose, Process and Practice: $6

The Song of Prayer: Prayer, Forgiveness, Healing: $6

The Gifts of God: $21

Concordance of *A Course in Miracles*: $49.95

Foundation for A Course in Miracles®
Dept. B
41397 Buecking Drive
Temecula, CA 92590

☐ I am interested in receiving a newsletter

☐ I am interested in receiving a catalog of books and tapes

☐ I am interested in receiving a schedule of workshops and classes

☐ Place me on your mailing list to receive your annual catalog and quarterly newsletter

PLEASE PRINT NEATLY

Name _____

Address _____

City, State, Zip _____